THE WRITING ON THE WALL
MEANT NOTHING TO ME

Bahareh Amidi

The Writing On The Wall Meant Nothing To Me

Copyright © 2025 Bahareh Amidi. All Rights Reserved.
ISBN 979-8-99262-406-9

cover and interior illustrations by
   Adora:
    @AdoraArts

email: connect@bahareh.com
facebook.com/Bahareh.Amidi
twitter.com/BaharehAmidi
youtube.com/baharehLIVE
instagram.com/bahareh_poetess
www.bahareh.com

"I came like water, and like wind I go."
— Omar Khayyam

Listen to The Writing On The Wall
Meant Nothing To Me

*It is as if I have woken up
in a jail cell and I look around
to find out what it all means
How can it be that
a princess in a glass castle on the clou*

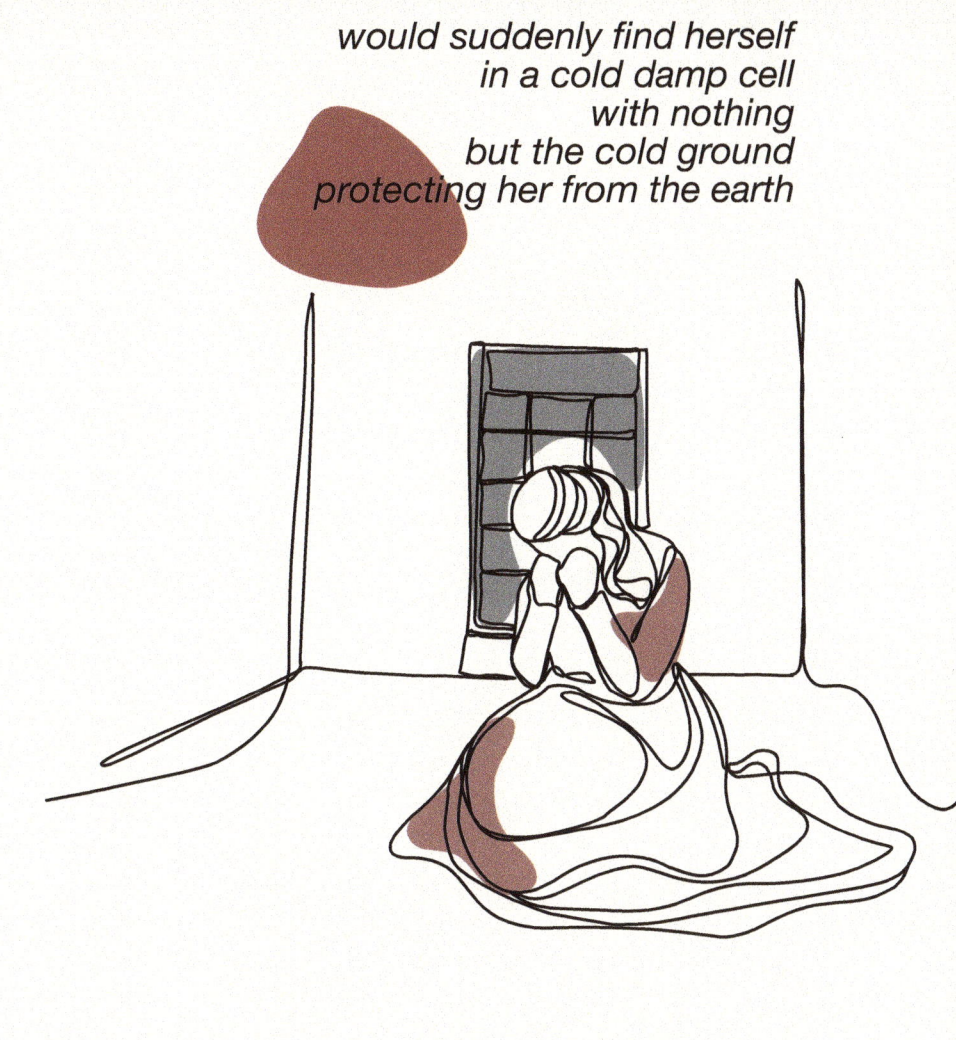

would suddenly find herself
in a cold damp cell
with nothing
but the cold ground
protecting her from the earth

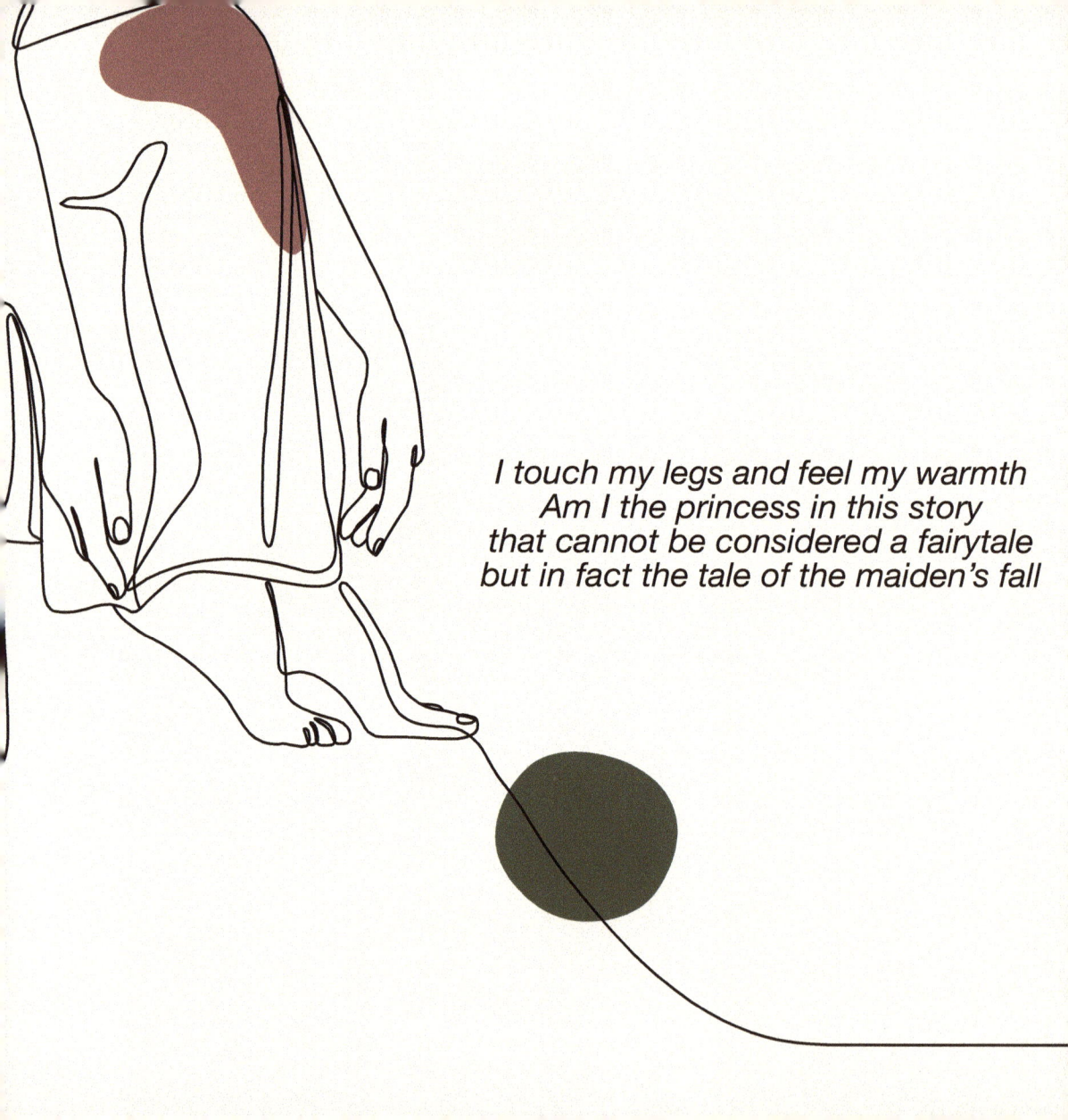

*I realize the reality of the situation
and I know I for one never believed in fairytales at all
The bleak realization of the truth pleases me
I smile but I do not cry*

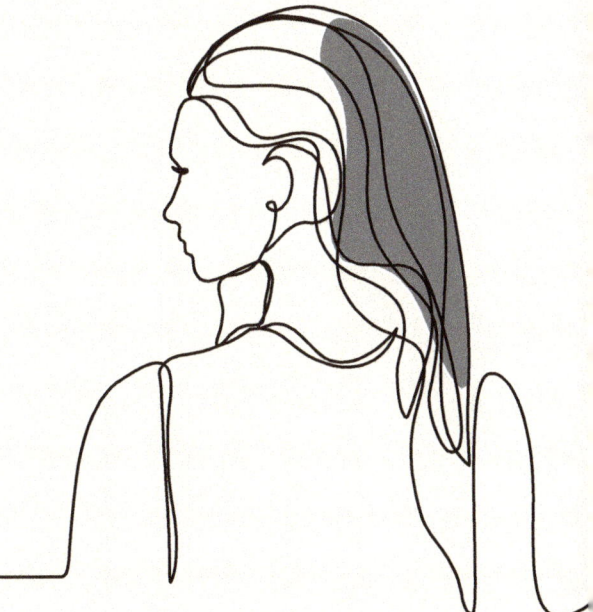

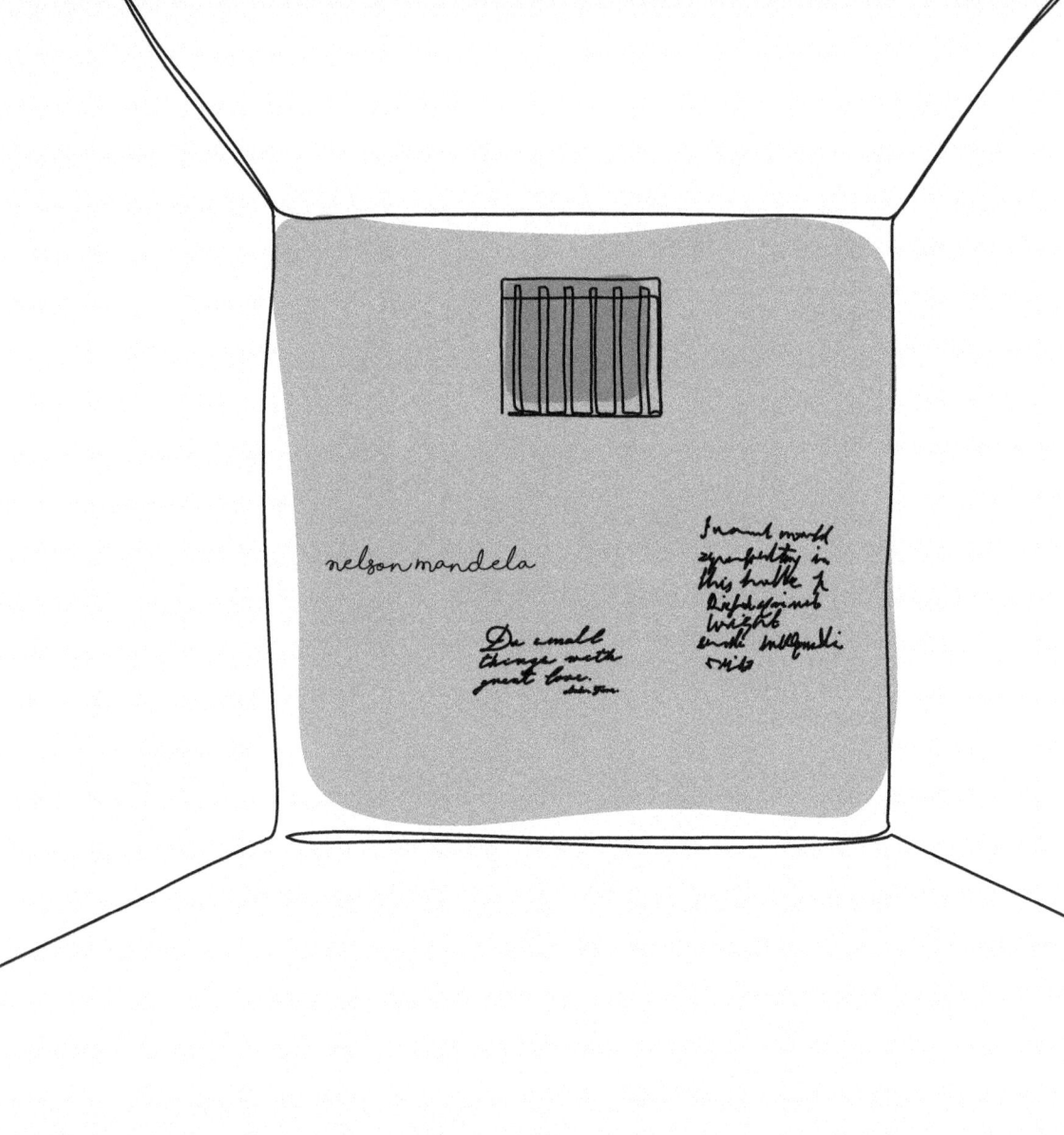

*Just as I rub my eyes
of the 44 centuries of sleep I have endured
I begin to realize
that there is writing on the walls of the cell I am in
I find that the cell mates
before me had each written a message on the wall
The first name I read is Nelson Mandela
then I recognize the frail hand of Gandhi
and the gentle handwriting of Mother Theresa
So many names so many eyes were here*

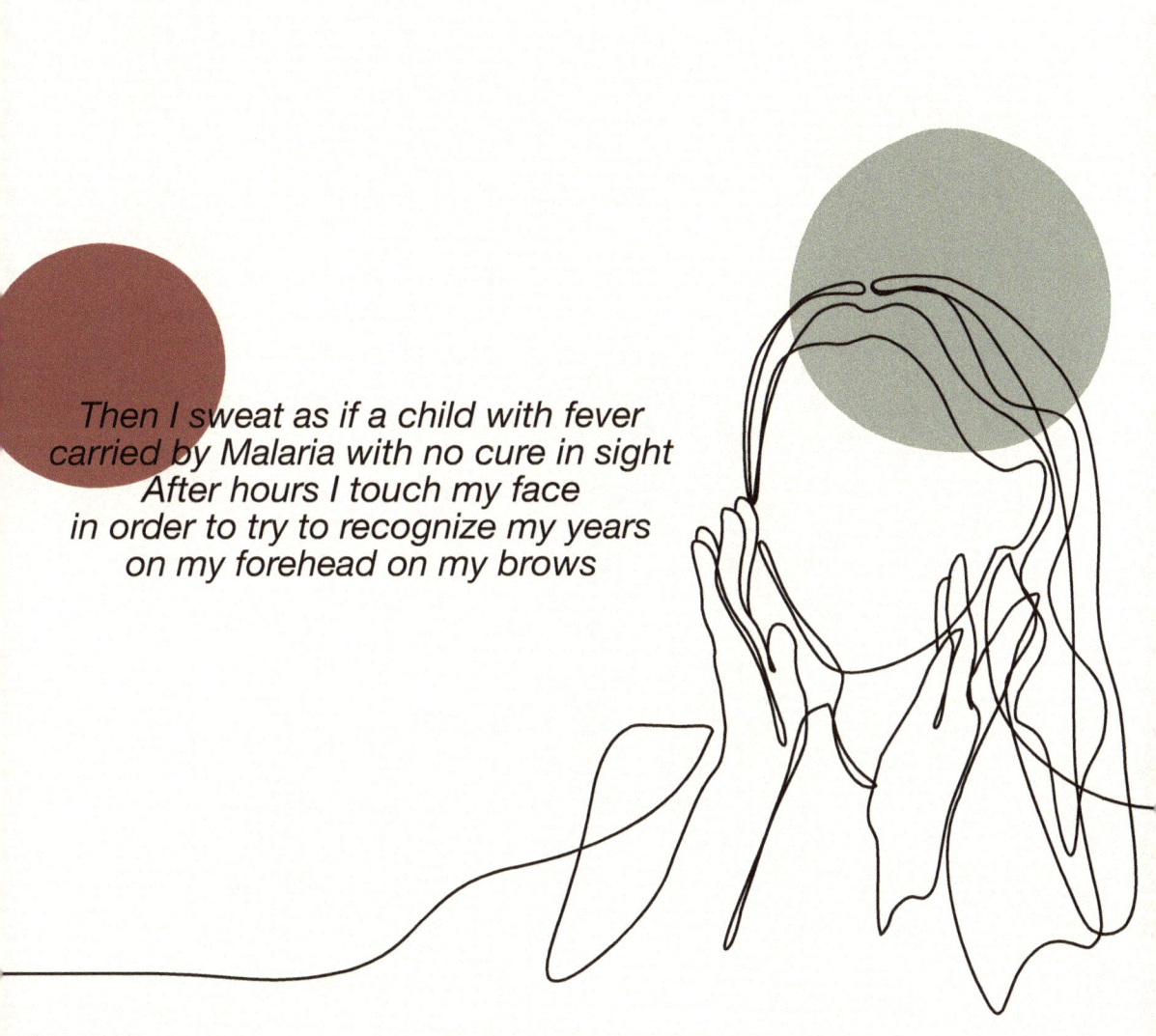

I look around the room
Now that I have identified myself
the cell feels more like a room
I see other names such as Hitler Stalin
and the man that stole from the beggar the other day
All these people saints in their own time
to some but disliked by many today
There was a piece of advice
from the good and the bad
Each saw the world
with their own eyes and each left a mark

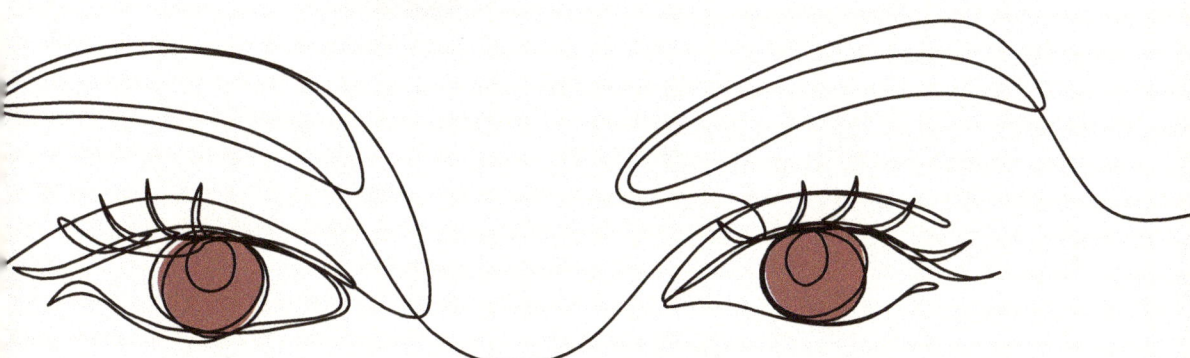

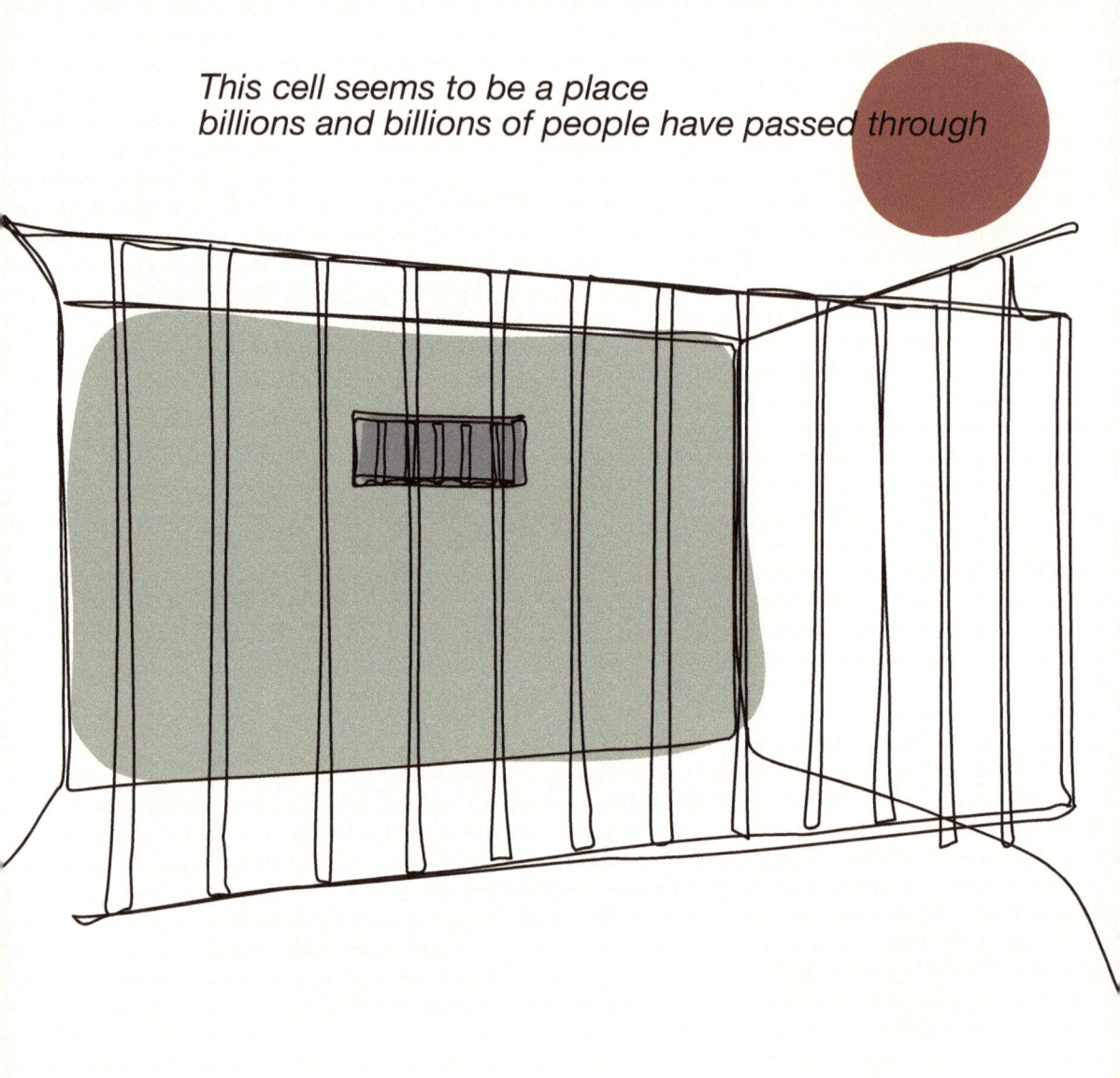

Some have changed the world
for the better and others have made it worse
So many have passed through without a trace
Perhaps those are the ones that came to life
ate gathered drank and took a breath in
but did not touch a life in any way
As I walk around the cell
I touch each of the words
and the peoples names

*It has taken me out of the glass castle
and helped me see
I have choice to go back
into the glass castle on the clouds
and never leave a footprint
or a writing on the wall
The decision takes no time at all*

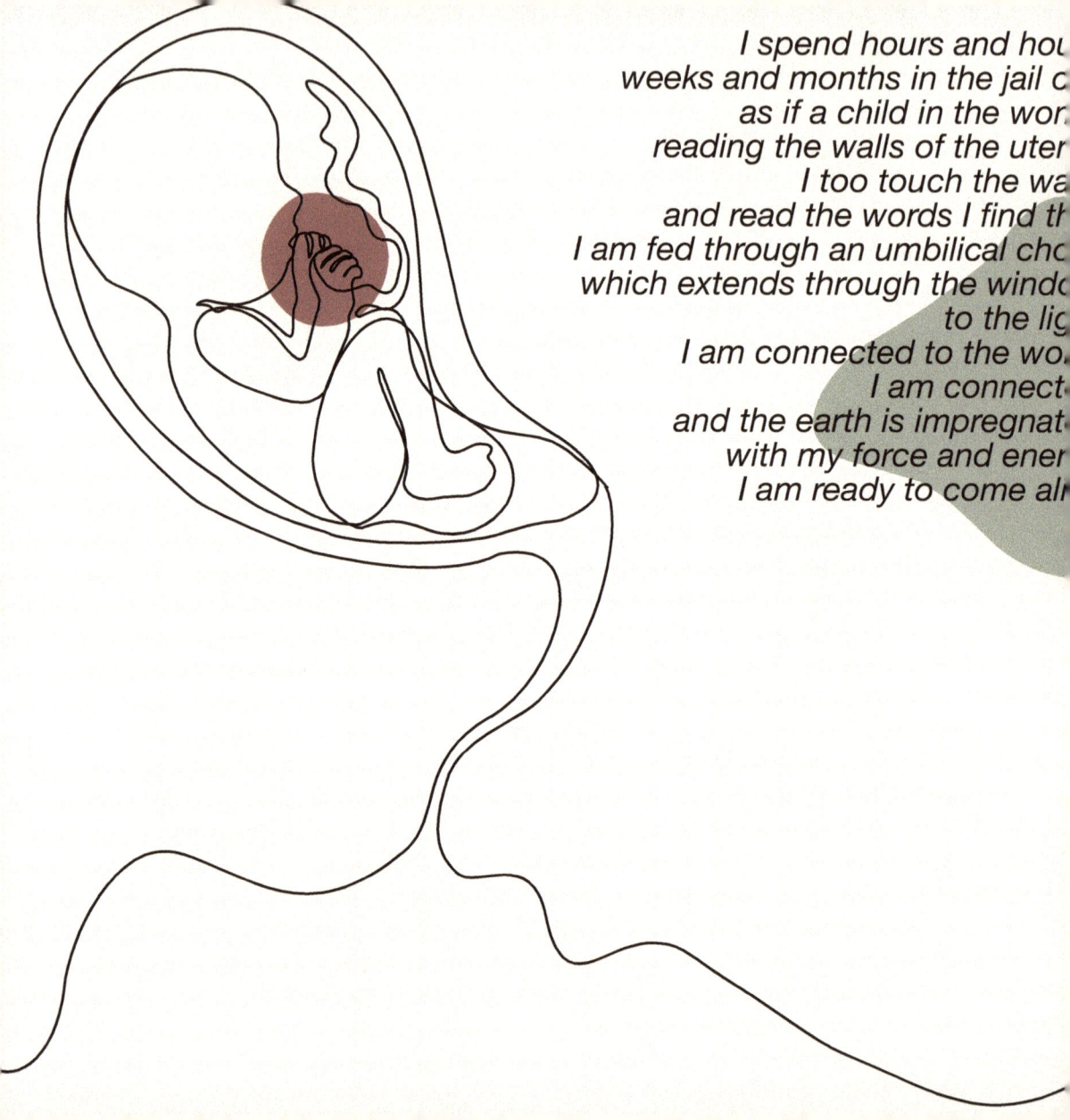

I spend hours and hou[rs]
weeks and months in the jail c[ell]
as if a child in the wor[ld]
reading the walls of the uter[us]
I too touch the wa[lls]
and read the words I find th[ere]
I am fed through an umbilical ch[ord]
which extends through the wind[ow]
to the lig[ht]
I am connected to the wo[rld]
I am connect[ed]
and the earth is impregnat[ed]
with my force and ener[gy]
I am ready to come al[ive]

*I know I do not want the glass castle on the clouds
After studying the millions
and millions of writings on the wall
I feel the answer in my heart
I know that I will offer something unique
to the world
I will not be a savious of one land
or one religion
I will not only work for women's rights
I will be the rainbow bridges
connecting sky to sea East to West
And faith and light to all*

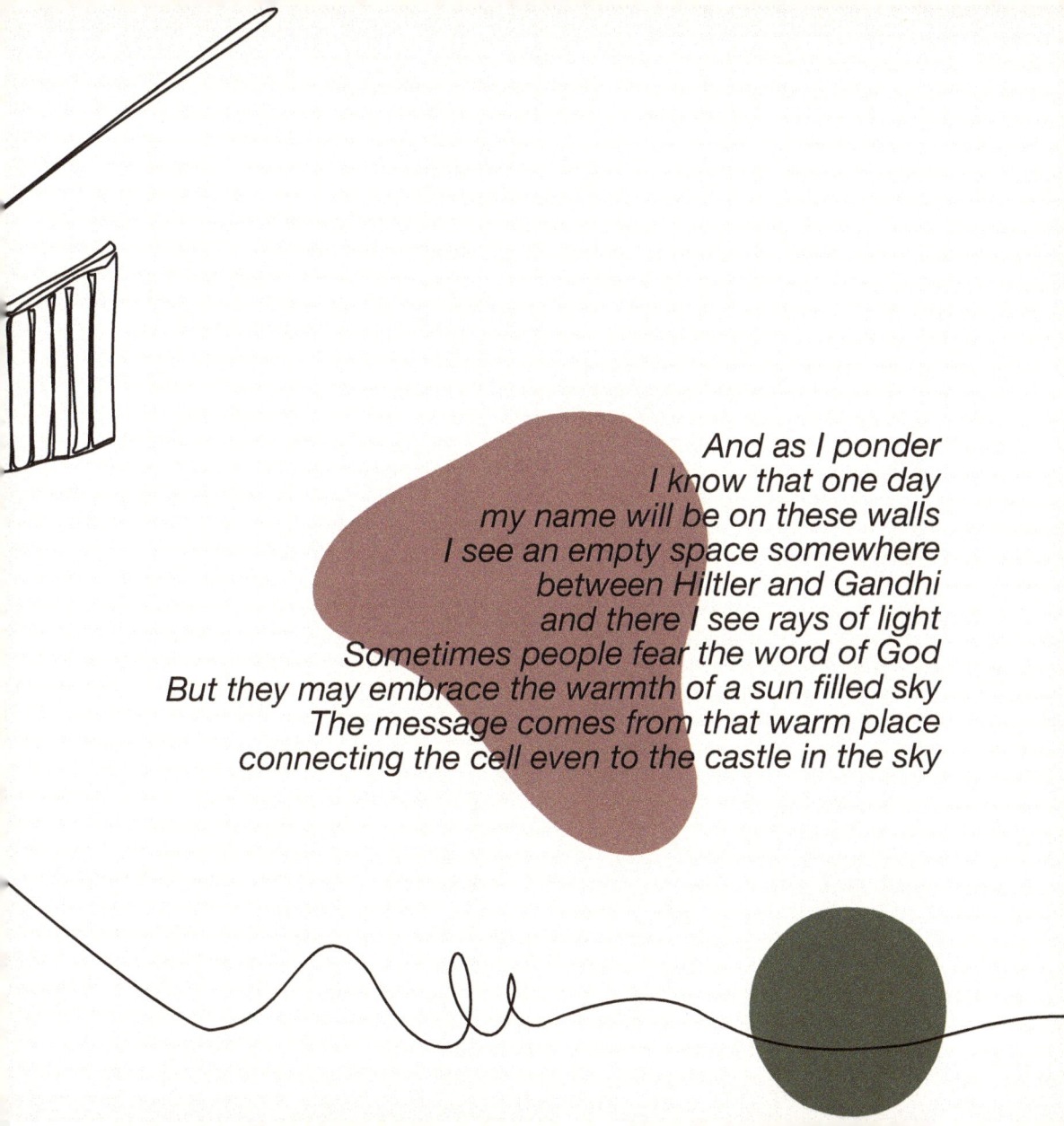

www.ingramcontent.com/pod-product-compliance
Lightning Source LLC
LaVergne TN
LVHW070529070526
838199LV00073B/6735